FeltCrafts® Needle Felting
Art Techniques and Projects

Anne Einset Vickrey

D1608620

Craft Works Publishing
Geneva, New York

Contributors Patricia Spark
Linda Van Alstyne

**Cover Art
and book Design** Linda R. Smith, Ithaca, NY

Photography Anne E. Vickrey
Patricia Spark
Linda Van Alstyne

Illustrations Linda R. Smith
Nina Ollikainen (sheep cartoons)

Editor Nancy K. Bereano

Library of Congress Cataloging-in-Publication Data

Vickrey, Anne Einset
    Needle felting art techniques and projects / Anne Einset Vickrey.
        p. cm.
    Includes bibliographical references.
    ISBN 0-9619053-2-8
     1. Felting. 2. Felt work. I. Title.

  TT849.5 .V5324 2002
  746'.0463--dc21

                                                        2002031239

10   9   8   7   6   5   4   3

Additional copies available from:
Craft Works Publishing
1-800-450-2723
www.feltcrafts.com

Contents

Introduction

The felting needle has been around for a long time but use of it as a sculptural tool is a fairly recent adaptation. I received my first felting needle from Patricia Spark in the late eighties and it went straight into my drawer and stayed there. I finally acquired an appreciation of how to work with it when Linda Van Alstyne gave me a brief lesson at the International Felt Festival in Norway in July, 2000. That fall, I took a class from Birgitte Krag Hansen, and the potential of this tool became clearer. Many artists have been employing felting needles for the last several years, developing new uses and techniques. Doll artists in particular have been extremely creative with needle felting.

Life-size fox made from karakul wool by Wendy Wiebe

This book presents the basics for beginning needle felting, starting with a discussion of the necessary materials. The book includes an in-depth look at the characteristics of felting needles and the various sizes preferred for needle felting techniques. Detailed instructions are given for flat felt and sculptural felt techniques. Basic and advanced techniques are included with pictorial techniques developed by Patricia Spark and sculptural techniques developed by Linda Van Alstyne. Included are two methods for building a face as well as techniques for combining wet and dry felting. A variety of project ideas are presented with the hope that you will build on these ideas to create your own unique artwork.

The goal of this book is to show the potential for using this tool on a variety of projects and how to get started. Begin with the simple projects, practicing with the needles, then build on your technique. You will be amazed at what you can create. Have fun!

CHAPTER 1

An Introduction to Needle or Dry Felting

What is Needle or Dry Felting?

Felt is a nonwoven material made up of fibers that lie randomly tangled or chemically bonded to each other so that they do not unravel. Most of us envision craft felt from kindergarten class when we think of felt.

Felt, however, can be made using wet or dry methods. Wet felting is when soap, water, and agitation causes animal fur or sheep's wool to form into felt fabric. Moisture and agitation is all that is needed to turn the wool into felt. This process is irreversible. That is, once you send a woolen sweater through the wash cycle of your washing machine it shrinks, never regaining its former size.

Dry felting is a much different process. Instead of using moisture and agitation, barbed needles are poked repeatedly into a pile of fibers, thereby entangling them until a flat piece of needle-felted material is achieved. Boot liners, felt gaskets, and acrylic craft felt are made in this manner. In industry, large beds of thousands of barbed needles are used to make needle-punched batting and fabric. Artists around the world make needle-punched wall hangings and rugs. Needle felting allows you to make flat felt or three-dimensional sculptural pieces.

Wet and dry felting techniques can be used together in many ways to create intricate sculptures, dolls, and decorative objects. Combining the two techniques in the same project opens up a wide range of possibilities to the artist. The felting needle can be used to add decoration, attach seams, and fix holes in felt made by the wet method. More innovative designs, techniques, and uses are developing as more artists are practicing needle felting.

Although this book's focus is dry felting, wet felting is discussed and suggested for several projects. To learn more about wet felting, look in the Appendix for suggestions for further reading.

The Felting Needle

To understand the process of dry felting let's first take a detailed look at the felting needle. The felting needle is not uniformly round like an ordinary sewing needle. The blade of the needle, which extends from the tip up ¾ inch, can be triangular, cross-shaped (star), or conical, with barbs going up the sides. The barbs are little notches in the needle that can barely be seen with the naked eye. They are shaped to hook the fibers as you push the needle into them, and to hold them, pulling them down and then letting the fibers go as the needle is pulled up. This action causes the fibers to entangle more and more as the needle is repeatedly pushed into them. After enough needle felting, the fibers will, by themselves, form a felt fabric. The felting needle is also used to poke fibers into a piece of fabric or batting. The fabric holds the fibers, allowing you to make designs on top.

There are literally hundreds of possible combinations of felting needles to use depending on the desired effect. The two most significant factors in dry felting are the gauge and the barb depth. The gauge of the needle tells its diameter. As the gauge number increases, the thickness of the needle decreases. The coarsest gauge most commonly used for dry felting is 36-gauge. One of the highest gauges, or finest needles, is 40-gauge. The lower gauge needles (36) will leave a more distinct hole in the felt if you use them for attaching the surface fiber. They are better suited to constructing the pieces of a figure. The higher gauge needle (40) gives you more control when making small details on a piece. Because it creates a smaller hole and allows more control in the amount of wool that is pushed into the piece, it causes less deformation of the surface of the piece as you use it.

The barb depth tells how deep the barb notch is. This makes all the difference in how much fiber is pushed down with each poke of the needle. A deeper barb will pull more wool down with each poke so pieces can be attached or felted more quickly. A smaller barb will require much more poking to get the same effect. The barb depth is graded on some needles. This means that the depth of the barb closest to the tip of the needle is smaller; the depth of the other barbs increases as you move up the blade. These differences in the needles make some better suited than others for particular techniques.

Needle felting artist, Linda Van Alstyne, researched different needles to find four that work best for her sculptural techniques. See "Overview of Felting Needles" in the Appendix. A description of these needles is given in Chapter 2, "Equipment and Materials."

ηeedle-Felting Techniques

There are four basic techniques for working with the felting needle. These are shallow poking and deep poking, and for sculptural work especially, the invisible attachment and the contouring or defining attachment. Remember as you work that felting needles are brittle. To insure a long life for your needles, poke the needle without bending it. Poke at an angle to the felt to get to hard to reach places.

Shallow Poking Versus Deep Poking with the Felting Needle The working portion of the felting needle is the blade with barbs going up the sides. The 38-gauge triangular blade needle and the 40-gauge triangular blade needle both have barbs that are graded where the barbs closest to the tip are shallower then the barbs going up the needle shaft. More delicate surface work can be done by poking shallowly with just the tip of the needle going $1/8$ to $1/4$ inch into the surface where less fiber is pushed in. Deep poking is when the needle is pushed two to three inches into the project, especially to attach two pieces or to needle felt a ball for a head of a figure. The needle is pushed into the project at one point and moved up and down without lifting the tip out of the project. With each up and down movement, more fibers are pushed from one piece into the adjoining piece. The 38-gauge triangular blade needle is used to attach parts of a figure together, securing the fibers from one piece into the adjoining piece. Deep poking can be used to give surface dimension by compacting the fibers deep within the figure to define muscles and other lines and proportions on the body. Because of the graded barbs on the 38-gauge needle, this needle is considered an all-purpose felting needle which can be used for both shallow and deep work.

The 38-gauge star blade needle has the same depth barb over the working part of the needle. The star blade has barbs on four surfaces versus the triangle blade that has barbs on three surfaces. This makes it ideal for shallow poking to needle felt the surface of a flat piece of felt or needle-felted figure.

Because of the equal depth barbs, and the additional surface, more fiber is pushed down with a shallower poke. Hold two or three of these needles together to go over the surface of your project, needle felting quickly without leaving needle marks.

Triangle

The 36-gauge triangular blade has deep barbs of the same depth over the working part of the needle so it pushes a lot of fiber down with each poke. It works well for attaching pieces using deep pokes and roughly needle-felting surfaces that will later be wet felted. The larger diameter of this needle leaves a more distinct hole in the surface and causes more deformity in the surface of the piece compared to the finer-gauge needles.

Seamless Attachment Versus Contouring Attachment As you gain more experience at needle felting and try sculptural techniques, you will find that attachments or shapes are added when building figures or faces with one of two attachment techniques: seamless or contouring.

A seamless attachment is used when you are adding a shape that you want to invisibly blend in with the piece. An example would be the top of the nose on a face. First you make the nose separately, needle felting it to hold its shape. An end of loose fiber is left on the top for attaching it to the face. To seamlessly attach the nose, place the nose on the face with the loose fiber fanning up toward the forehead area. Poke your felting needle into the wool at an angle parallel to the loose fibers of the nose, pointing toward the forehead in the same direction that the fibers are lying. The barbs on the needle will catch the wool and push it into the surface of the face invisibly. Once the fibers are caught, poke shallowly with the 38-gauge star or 40-gauge needle, going perpendicular to the surface to secure the attachment. Attaching shapes in this way gives a blind edge to your attachment.

A contouring attachment is when you are giving a defined edge to an attachment. The bottom of the nose is an example of this. Poke your needle more perpendicularly to the fiber so that it makes a line along the bottom of the nose where it attaches to the face. Make another line on each side of the nose to define the nostrils. The kneecap is another example of an attachment where the top is meshed in with a seamless attachment and the bottom can be defined with a line under the kneecap.

Safety Tips for Working with Felting Needles

Felting needles are very sharp, so needle felting is recommended only for adults and children 12 and up. You can accidentally poke yourself because you may have to hold your project with one hand while the other hand is poking it with a needle.

1. **Wear latex finger protectors** (See "Sources" in Appendix) on the hand that is not holding the needle as you are learning, or wear a heavy rubber glove. If poked hard enough, the needle will go through the glove so care should be taken not to stab with the needle.

2. **Make a place where you can hold the needle** Tear off an 18-inch piece of $1/2$-inch masking tape. Wrap the tape around the top of the needle just underneath the bend. Hold the needle at the tape and write the needle size on the tape. Tape two or three of the same length needles together for faster felting when you are adding a covering layer or finishing a flat piece.

3. **Always work on a foam work surface that is large enough for your project** A 10 x 10-inch surface that is at least 1-inch thick is a good size. When making flat felt, the needle goes through the wool and into the foam. The needle should only go $1/8$ to $1/4$-inch deep into the foam.

4. **As long as you keep your hand that isn't holding the needle away from the needle, you will not poke yourself** Below are some ways to do that.

- Hold the needle in one hand and hold the side of the work surface with the other hand.

- Keep your eyes on the needle as you poke.

- For three-dimensional felt, tack your project down to the work surface with a large sewing needle or a thin knitting needle.

- Always know where your needle is.

- When you pause, stick the needle into the foam work surface.

- When you stop, place the needle in its holder.

- Keep the needles away from small children.

- Always look where you are poking. **If you look away...STOP POKING!**

- If you accidentally break a needle, pick up the sharp pieces with the sticky side of a piece of tape and dispose of them properly.

Equipment & Materials

*Needle felting supplies are available from a variety of sources.
Some of these are included in the Appendix.*

Felting Needles Below are the four needle sizes referred to in this book. Each one has particular advantages. Practice using the various needles in the following projects to see which ones work best for different needle felting purposes.

- **36-gauge triangular blade** 3.5-inch needle with equal depth barbs beginning $^3/_8$th inch from tip.
- **38-gauge triangular blade** 3.5-inch needle with varied barb depth beginning 3.2mm from tip.
- **38-gauge star blade** 3-inch needle with shallow barbs of equal depth beginning 3.2mm from tip.
- **40-gauge triangular blade** 3-inch needle with varied barb depths from shallow to somewhat deeper beginning 3.2mm from tip.

Multi-Needle Tools There are a variety of multi-needle tools available for needle felting. These tools hold two or more needles at once. They are especially useful when you are needle felting a large flat area as described in the section on "Pictorial Felt" by Patricia Spark. For smaller pieces, you can make your own tool by taping two or three needles together, or by taping them to a small stick.

Work Surface You need to work on a spongy surface when needle felting. The foam protects the needles from breaking and protects you from being poked. The foam or sponge should give some resistance to the needle so that the needle doesn't poke through it easily. Many products can be used, including Styrofoam, cellulose sponges, foam rubber and foam packing materials. Try to save foam packing material to use for needle felting, especially the gray foam used to cushion electronic equipment.

Fiber Dry felting differs from wet felting in that any type of fiber can be used in the former. Wool fleece is the fiber recommended for the projects in this book. The advantage to using wool is that it can be wet felted, and sheep's wool is easy to obtain in a myriad of colors. The felting needles recommended here work well with wool fiber. If you are unfamiliar with the terms used to describe wool fiber, read the definitions in the Appendix for "Wool-Related Vocabulary" used in this book.

Different sheep breeds supply wool whose qualities are suitable for different purposes in needle felting. Below are suggestions for fiber choice.

Core Fiber For the inside, or core, of three-dimensional sculptures, a downy or spongy wool that holds its loft works best. This type of wool is found on sheep that are raised for their meat rather than for their wool. The wool compacts much less when it is needled than wool from breeds whose wool felts easily using the wet felt techniques. Some breeds to use for core wool are: Dorset, Southdown, Hampshire, Cheviot, and Suffolk.

Cover Fiber A medium/coarse wool is less likely to show the tiny holes that the felting needles make. This is more important when making an entirely needle felted sculpture. If needle marks are showing on a project, the surface can be wet felted to smooth the surface. For finely detailed pictorial felt, medium/fine or fine fibers work well if used with fine needles, again wet felting after the needle felting helps fill in the holes.

Specialty Fibers Ideas for decorating your needle-felted sculptures are limitless. Dressing your project with fabric or wet-felted clothing makes it completely original. Locks of wool from curly sheep breeds or mohair goats can be dyed and used for hair. Heat-bondable iridescent fibers can be used for hair, clothing, or wings. Silk or manufactured fibers can be needled or wet felted between wool fibers onto your project.

Yarn Hairy or loosely spun yarns are best for needling onto the surface of your project.

Fabric Try needle punching into a variety of fabrics using different needle sizes to see which works best. You want a needle that pushes more fiber down but doesn't distort the fabric. Cotton batting, which is a needle-punched fabric, allows the needle to go through it easily. It is available where fabric is sold. Needle-punched merino wool quilt batt can be used. Patricia Spark's wall pieces often use this pre-felt fabric as a base. Felt scrim, a stiff woven material that has been felted, gives a stiff backing for making pins. It is available at fabric stores and is generally used as the backing for varsity letters. Even very thin fabrics such as cotton gauze or voile can be needle felted using the proper needle.

Flat Needle-Felting Techniques

If you have no experience with needle felting, begin by practicing with these first two projects. Here are two ways to make flat-needled felt. The first way is to needle punch into fabric. The second way is to needle punch directly onto the foam work surface.

Make Felt by Needle-Felting onto a Background Fabric

Use this technique to needle pictures or three-dimensional sculptures onto clothing or fabric, and to make masks and pins.

Use the 40-gauge and 38-gauge star needles because they will leave the smallest holes on top of the needled fabric. Hold the needle just under the bend with your thumb, index finger, and middle finger. Rest your arm on the work surface and poke the needle into the wool, flexing at the wrist or elbow. ♥

8

PROJECT 1 Needle Felt a Heart Shape

Materials One-tenth ounce of red wool. A 4" x 4" piece of fabric. Needles and foam work surface. A felt marker.

1. Place your foam work surface on a table and place a small piece of cotton batting or soft fabric on top.

2. Draw a heart shape on one side of the batting with a felt marker.

3. Place a tuft of red wool on the inside of the heart and poke it into the batting using the 40-gauge felting needle. Hold the needle straight up and down and poke it into the wool and batting going only $1/8$ to $1/4$ inch into the foam. As you poke, some of the fibers will be buried in the foam. This holds the project in place as you work. Pull off more small tufts of wool and poke them into the batting until you have covered the outlined heart.

Poke the needle straight into the wool for several minutes. As you work, notice how the wool becomes flatter and stiffer. Keep poking until you have an evenly felted surface on the heart. (Make the needle felting go more quickly by holding two or three needles at a time.)

Some Ideas for Finishing the Heart

- Cut around the heart and sew on a piece of yarn to make a necklace.

- Needle a message with contrasting wool onto the heart then glue a magnet to the back for a refrigerator magnet.

- Cut a hole in the middle and place a picture behind it. You have a picture frame.

Try needle punching designs onto fabric to make sculptural pins

- **Lamb** Needle punch white wool in a lamb shape. Cut around the lamb close to the wool. Make an ear and tail separately and needle them on. Add a black eye, then glue or sew a pin onto the back.

- **Pig** Make in the same way as the lamb.

- **Teapot** Needle punch a teapot design onto stiff felt scrim. Outline it and cut around the design. Add a pin to the back. ☺

Basset Hound on denim jacket by Wendy Wiebe

Masks can be made by needle punching into a background fabric. Instructions for simple masks for Halloween or drama can be found in Chapter 6.

Make Flat Felt by Needling onto a Foam Work Surface

When you needle felt directly onto a foam work surface you can wet felt the piece after you have arranged the wool. In this way you have more control over your design than if you layered the wool and only wet felt it. As you needle over the work surface, some of the fibers become buried in the foam and serve to hold your project in place as you are working on it. When you are finished, gently pull the dry felt off of the work surface to keep it in one piece. Let's try a simple project to get the idea of this technique. ★

PROJECT 2 Needle Felt a Star Shape

Materials One-quarter ounce of yellow wool.
Needles and foam work surface.

1. Trace a star onto a piece of paper and cut it out.
Layer a pile of wool on top of the foam.
Place the paper star on top of the wool.
Use the 38-gauge felting needle and poke
around the outside border of the star
shape on top of the wool. Keep poking on
the same line until you have an indentation in the wool.

2. Take away the paper shape and fold the wool that is outside the line over
the line toward the inside of the star. Poke the felting needle two or three times into the folded
wool to tack down one fold at a time. Add some more wool to the middle of the star where the
fiber is thinner. Hold two or three needles and poke over the star until it is flattened. Gently lift
the star from the work surface and turn it over.

3. Needle felt the other side, angling the needle so it does not poke through
the
star. Soon you will have a stiff, flat piece of felt. You can add
more
wool to
spots
that are
too thin.
Needle a
face
onto the
star.

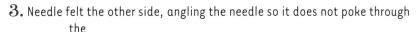

Doll house rug, needle felted in coarse wool then wet felted.

Wet Felting Technique for Needle-Felted Projects

Wet felting the surface of a needle-felted project will make the surface smooth. Practice on the star. Place a bar of soap and a bowl of warm water next to you. Wet your fingers and rub them on the soap, then rub one spot on the star until the fibers lie flat. Gently rub that spot for half a minute then repeat over the entire surface of the star. Wet your fingers as you work. The surface should not be sudsy. After the front of the star is felted, work on the back. Gently rub both sides of the star for several minutes to wet felt the surface. Let the star dry, then rinse it under a gentle water spray and hang it up to dry. You can use the star as an ornament. ◆

Pictorial Felting Techniques with Patricia Spark

Patricia Spark developed the following technique for making pictorial felt. This method has many applications. It is a great example of how combining wet and dry felting techniques can result in wonderful works of fiber art. Pictorial felt designs on pages 14-20 by Patricia Spark.

Needling Onto a Pre-Felted Background

There are many ways to make pictures in feltmaking. An easy way for beginners is to use pre-felt (explained below) as the background for the picture. Students can make their own pre-felt or they can use a merino quilt batt. These batts are made on a needle-felting machine. Designing on these white batts is like designing on paper.

Make a Pre-Felt

The terms pre-felt, soft-felt, and half-felt mean the same thing. A pre-felt is a piece of felt which is still soft enough to be attached to more fleece. This means it has enough loose fibers available to tangle with the new fleece. Designs can be cut out of the pre-felt and then laid on a background of fleece or other pre-felts. The coarser the fiber, the softer the pre-felt needs to be in order to be attachable. I like to use fine merino wool fiber for my pre-felts. It makes a firmer, more detailed pre-felt which will still attach to a fleece ground. This helps give a more accurate design.

- Use one ounce of fiber for every square foot of pre-felt. Pre-felt should be $3/8$" thick.

- For a pre-felt made by the wet method, work on a waterproof surface.

- For a pre-felt made by the dry method, work on a piece of foam rubber.

- Try making the pre-felt out of many different colors of wool. Use a color gradation, or create an image by using bits of different colors.

Dry Method for Making the Pre-Felt

1. Put a thin layer of the carded fleece on a foam rubber mat covering the area you have planned for the pre-felt. Overlap the pieces of carded fleece slightly to create an even layer of wool. Place a second layer on top of the first with the fibers lying crosswise to the first layer. Make many thin layers rather than a few thicker ones. Continue adding layers, alternating the directions of the layers, until the entire weighed fleece has been used.

2. Punch the fleece with a felting needle until it begins to tangle together. Using a multi-needle tool that holds five or six needles at once lets you cover the punching area more quickly.

3. Continue punching until the whole pre-felt is holding together well. Peel the pre-felt off the foam rubber. If the pre-felt is made of medium to coarse wool it will peel off easily and hold together well. If it is fine fiber, such as merino, you might have to peel the pre-felt off the foam rubber and roll it a few times (maybe fifteen rotations from each side) using the wet method described below. Otherwise it will require much more punching.

Wet Method for Making the Pre-Felt

1. Lay out a piece of bubble wrap (smooth side up) that is approximately 2 inches wider and 6 inches longer than your planned pre-felt. Place a thin layer of the carded fleece on top of the bubble wrap in the area you want the pre-felt. Add layers in the same way described in "Dry Method for Making a Pre-felt" above. Overlap the pieces of carded fleece slightly so that an even layer of wool will be created. Do not make the layer too thick. It is better to have many thin layers than to have a few thick ones. Lay down enough fleece to cover the area you have planned. Place the second layer on top of the first with the fibers lying crosswise to the first layer. Continue alternating the directions of the layers until the entire weighed fleece has been used.

2. Place a piece of netting (*e.g.,* mosquito net) on top of the wool pile. The net prevents the wool from sticking to the sponge as you apply the water. Apply lukewarm soapy water with a sponge to the wool stack, wetting it all down so all the fiber is moist and the pile flattened. There should be no air bubbles left in the pile. The fiber does not need to be dripping wet, just moist and flat.

3. Lift the net off of the pre-felt and fold over the edges of the pre-felt about $\frac{1}{2}$ inch, for straight edges. Apply another thin layer of fiber if necessary to build up thin areas. Re-apply the net and wet down any new fiber.

4. Roll the wool in bubble wrap to felt it.
- Lay a rolling bar on one end of the bubble wrap then roll up the wool "sandwich" leaving the net on top of the fleece. I like a $1\frac{1}{2}$" diameter PVC pipe for my rolling bar, but a wooden closet pole works well too.

- Tie the roll in several places. A neat trick is to use cotton/lycra stretch fabric to make your ties. It "snugs" up well to the roll.

- Using your forearms or your feet, rotate the roll back and forth, with light pressure fifty times. Unroll and lift up on the net to make sure it isn't attached to the wool. Smooth out any wrinkles.

- Re-roll the "sandwich" from the opposite end. Rotate fifty times again and unroll.

- If the piece is not too long for the width of the bubble wrap, turn the felt sideways and roll it fifty times in that direction. Repeat with 50 rolls from the opposite side so that all four directions have been rolled 50 times. If it is too large to turn, just roll it from the opposite ends again.

- Check the pre-felt by placing it in a towel and wringing out the water. Look at the felt. If it is barely holding together, it needs another round of rolling. If it is a pretty good sheet, but still slightly fluffy, it's what you want. Is it really firm, not fuzzy at all? Oops! You've probably gone too far. If your fiber choice was Merino, it will usually be OK, but if you chose a coarser fiber, there may not be enough fibers left to tangle with the fleece background. ❀

Make a Design on the Pre-felt

Work out a possible design on paper. If you can't think of your own design, you can look at photographs, embroidery design books, stencil books, decorative painting books, etc. for ideas. The design cannot be too complicated. After you've tried one of these wall hangings, you will see that it is not possible to make something that is really intricate.

Materials Foam rubber sheet 3-5 inches on all sides larger than the wall hanging.

Felting Needles: Choose the correct needle size/type for the fiber that is chosen. When I am using Merino, or even the slightly coarser Corriedale, I like to use the 38-gauge, triangular needle with the notches that start approximately 3.2mm from the tip. When using a coarser fiber such as Romney, or even the rug fleece, Karakul, I like to use a 36-gauge triangular needle with the notches starting approximately $3/8$ inch from the tip. Normally I use 38-gauge triangle for "roughing in" the design shapes and 38-gauge star for detail work.

Wool Fleece in Different Colors that Felts Well: A fine fiber allows more detail. With a coarse fiber, I have to simplify the design. The wool is strengthened by wet felting afterwards. Fleece that doesn't felt well by wet methods can be tangled together well with the felting needles.

Fuzzy or Softly Spun Yarns: Yarns are good for adding lines to a design. With some practice, they can even be used for making words.

Equipment for Wet Felting: Cellulose sponge, Nylon mosquito net several inches larger than the starting size of the project, Bar of glycerin or olive oil soap, Cloth towel, Rolling bar (1½" PVC pipe or wooden closet pole, wider than wall hanging), Sheet of small size (³⁄₈") bubble wrap (3-5 inches bigger than wall hanging), Strips of rag (stretchy cotton-lycra fabric), about 1" x 18", Gallon bucket for water.

Hold yarn loosely when needling onto design.

Place the Design Lay the dry pre-felt on the sheet of foam rubber and figure out where the design is going to be. There are several ways to do this.

1. **Using Yarn Outlines as a Guide** Lay yarn down on the pre-felt and "draw" the outlines of the shapes with it. After the yarn is in place, you can use the felting needle to baste it down into position. (Hold the length of yarn in one hand and needle it down with the other. The yarn needs to be longer than you'd think, since it draws in as it's being needled. Don't cut it off until the entire shape is outlined.) Once the shapes are outlined, you can needle colored fleece into the outlined areas. This is much like filling in a page of a coloring book.

Flower center was shaped by laying down fleece and placing a paper shape on top. A line of indentation was needled around the paper shape.

2. **Using Cut Paper Shapes as a Guide** Cut out shapes in paper. Then lay these shapes down on the background and arrange them until the composition is pleasing. When they are in place, use the yarn to outline the shapes, then remove the paper. Fill in the outlined shapes by needling colored fleece into them. You can also lay a bit of colored fleece under the shape and needle around the outside edge of the shape to make a line indentation. Then remove the paper shape and fold the wool fringes in towards the shape and needle them down.

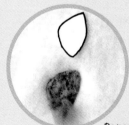

3. **Using Stencils as a Guide** Lay the stencil over the pre-felt and needle fleece in the open area, thus filling in the shape.

Paper removed, then fleece fringe folded back over indented line and needled.

4. Working Directly, without a Guide There are a couple of different ways to design directly onto the pre-felt background.

- Cut shapes out of pre-felts. Make pre-felts out of many different colors so you have a "pallet" of colors to choose from. Use a dog brush to roughen up the backside of the shape and then lay this rough side down on the pre-felt background. Needle the shape into position.

- Lay colored fleece down onto the background and needle it into position. Depending on how much fleece you needle down, the shape will be opaque or transparent (with background showing through).

Attach the Design Needle the shapes into position on the pre-felt ground. Use the felting needles to baste the shape first by jabbing it down a few places in the middle. Finally, carefully needle around the edge of the shape, making sure that it is holding down well.

Hold the foam mat up so that you can see the design clearly. Stand away from it and squint. Any shapes that are too dominant will jump out at you. Does this dominance disturb the balance of the composition? Or does it make it more interesting? If it is disturbing, you can easily pull the shape off the background and put another shape or color there instead. This is a lot like using an eraser to remove unwanted areas of a drawing, only less messy!

After the composition is the way you want it, needle it a little more to make sure that everything is holding on well, then carefully peel the wall hanging off the foam mat. I gently pull, and roll up the pre-felt as I'm going in order to get it off the mat without mishaps.

Flower image needled onto merino quilt batt background. Petals, leaves, and stem cut from pre-felts while other parts are made from fleece.

Needle held at an angle to attach pre-felt appliqué.

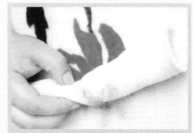

Pre-felt is carefully peeled off of the foam rubber for wet felting.

Wet Felt the Design

If the wool is a type that can be felted by the wet method, you should now felt it a bit to "set" the design. This will prevent the shapes from being pulled off. To do this:

1. Lay the wall hanging on the piece of bubble wrap, bubble side up.

2. Put the bar of glycerin soap into warm water and swish it around until the water looks milky. Sponge this soapy water over the wall hanging until all of the wool is well saturated. You will need more soapy water with coarse wool than with fine wool.

3. Lay the rolling bar on one end of the bubble wrap and roll it up with the wall hanging, making sure that the rolling bar does not actually touch the wall hanging. Try to have one turn of bubble wrap around the bar before the wall hanging starts. Tie the roll in a few places with the rag strips.

The rolled up pre-felt tied and ready for rotating.

4. Rotate the roll back and forth with your forearms or your feet, thirty times. Unroll the bundle and place the rolling bar on the other end of the wall hanging. Roll it up again and rotate another thirty times. (The area against the rolling bar will felt more tightly, so it is best to alternate ends to achieve even felting.)

5. Unroll the bundle and give the wall hanging a quarter turn. Re-roll and rotate thirty times. Re-roll from the other end and rotate thirty times. Now you should have rolled it from all four sides. Depending on the fleece used and how hard the felt skin you want, you might be able to stop now. If the felt feels too loose, roll and rotate the bundle from the four sides again. But increase the rotations to fifty times each side and turn the felt over so that you are rolling it from the backside.

6. Test for Felting "Doneness." Push on the fibers on the surface of the wall hanging. Do they shift or stay in place? If they shift, you need to roll it more. If they are tightly in place, you can stop. Gently rinse the soap out of the wall hanging and soak it in a vinegar solution for 15 minutes ($1/4$ cup white vinegar to 1 quart water). Rinse out the vinegar solution. Lay out the wall hanging on a towel to dry. You can block its shape by stretching and patting it into position.

Chapter 4

Sculptural Needle-Felting Techniques

To make a needle-felted figure you start with its parts - the basic shapes that will comprise the figure. These are usually formed from core wool and then attached together. The cover fiber can be added either before or after the parts are attached. The sculptural detail is created using cover fiber that builds on the surface, as in clay modeling.

To make a shape, start with a strip of carded wool. Place several thin layers on top of each other or start with one layer depending on the size of the shape you are hoping to achieve. These strips of wool are also referred to as batts in some sections of the book.

Make Basic Shapes

The goal when making the shapes for your figure is to roll the wool snugly and evenly. More control can be achieved if you roll the fiber on top of your foam work surface. Always roll the fiber strips, or batts, from tip to tip. Once the shape is rolled up hold it tightly when needling it. Avoid poking the needle through the shape and out the other side. Needle the shapes with deep pokes while rotating so the surface is not needled too much and the shape is not flattened. The basic shapes will be needled more when attached to other shapes and when cover fiber is added. Excessive needling of the basic shape will create a hard surface. This will make it difficult to attach cover fiber and add sculptural detail to the pieces. Use the longer needles, 36-gauge and 38-gauge triangular blade, to form the basic shapes.

Roll batt from tip to tip.

Cylinder or Tube Shape (for arms and legs of a figure)

Start with carded core fiber. Place the fiber on your foam work surface extending out in front of you. Start rolling from one end. Beginning with the very end fibers, roll with a tight even tension. After the wool is rolled up, needle the ends of the strip to the shape. Be careful to hold the shape while needle felting the fibers. Wool has energy in it. If you release your grasp on the shape, it will spring or release and the firmness of the shape will be lost. Poke the 38-gauge triangular needle into the roll several times to hold its shape. Leave the fibers at each end loose (not needled) if you are attaching the roll to another piece.

Long Cord (for a tail or snake)
Place the strip of carded wool at an angle in front of you. Roll away from you at an angle to the strip, working up the strip as you form a long cord. Needle the roll so it will hold its shape. To make a longer cord, overlap with another strip of wool before you reach the end. Make a thicker cord by starting with a thicker layer of wool.

Needle the roll to secure it.

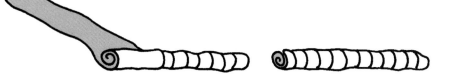

Oval Shape (for a head or body) Place a strip of wool on your work surface. Place another strip down the middle to make a thicker layer. Begin rolling and folding the sides over the middle as you roll. When you reach the end, needle the loose ends into the oval. Needle the oval with deep pokes, rotating it to form an oval shape, working looser areas onto the shape. Practice this technique by making an oval then covering it with colored wool to make a decorated egg.

Ball Shape (for a head or body) Start the same way as you would for the oval, turning in the wool at the sides as you roll. When you have rolled half-way up the strip, roll the ball sideways for a half roll, then continue to roll it straight up the strip. Needle the loose ends. Needle the ball with deep pokes as you continue rotating it to make it round.

Cone Shape (for horns or body) Lay the strip of core wool in front of you. Add more fiber on one side of the strip. Starting from one end, roll up the strip rolling more tightly on the side that has the lesser amount of wool. Needle the cone while rotating it, especially at the tip. If you are using the cone shape for horns or other embellishments, leave the fibers at the base of the cone shape loose so that it can easily be attached to the figure. If using the cone shape for the trunk of a body, needle the loose fibers into the base of the cone.

Needle ends of roll to shorten.

You can form cone shapes by wrapping wool onto a bamboo skewer or thin wooden dowel. Start wrapping 1/2 inch from the tip of the skewer. Wrap toward the tip and back, gradually building up the wool to the size you want. Build up the thicker part of the cone last. Carefully needle the wool before sliding it off of the skewer.

Adjust the Basic Shapes If a shape is too long, needling at the ends can shorten it. Place the shape on its side on top of the sponge. Hold the shape and carefully push the needle horizontally into one end of the shape. Move the needle in and out with deep jabs. This action will shorten the piece. You can work both ends in the same manner.

You can alter one of the basic shapes by adding more wool in a particular area, rolling it over another strip of wool, or wrapping a strip of wool evenly over the area and then needling it down.

Building a Figure

An infinite variety
of figures can be made
using the basic shapes and
needle felting techniques.
Lay out the shapes you made to
form a figure. Keep in mind the pose
the figure will have as you connect the parts.
Combining different shapes can form unique figures.
Adding the cover fiber hides the attachments to give the effect
of a solid figure. 🐻 Detail can be added after the figure
is constructed and additional shapes made from the cover
fiber wool applied for more features. Because the head
is usually the most detailed piece of a figure, it is
attached last after the figure is constructed so
that it maintains its shape and detail.

Cuddly Bear by Linda Van Alstyne

Brown-Bear An Animal with a Core & Needle-Felted Skin

Instructions for this are for a simple bear figure. A bear can be made in many ways by changing the pose, the shape of the body, etc. Follow the steps for constructing a figure and use your imagination and creativity to make the figure unique.

Materials All four needle sizes. Foam work surface. Core and cover fiber amounts depend on the size of the bear. With paper and pencil, draw the bear and the parts to get an idea of the dimensions and how they fit together.

Roll the Basic Shapes Start with core wool. Pull off strips of equal size for two legs and for two arms. Roll two cylinder/tube shapes of equal size for the legs. Roll two cylinder/tube shapes of equal size for the arms. Make an oval for the body.

When you have completed the pieces, you can cover them individually with the cover fiber before you attach the pieces together. Or you can attach the pieces and add the cover fiber afterwards. The first choice may be easier for beginners. Take strips of the cover fiber and needle one end to a shape. Gently stretch the rest of the strip around the piece, needling every inch to hold it down. Be sure the fiber is flat to the piece as you needle it down.

Construct the Arms, Legs and Body Together Arrange the bear parts on top of the foam. Place the arms together on top of the body as shown. Poke the 36- or 38-gauge needle at an angle through one arm and deep into the body but not through the body. You are attaching the arm by pushing some of the fibers from the arm deep into the body to attach the two together. Move the needle up and down inside the body, pulling the working part of the needle up high enough to catch more of the fibers in the end of the arm but not pulling the point out of the wool.

25

After five up and down motions, lift the needle out of the wool and poke it into another spot on the top of the arm. Repeat in three spots until the arms are secured to the body. Place the needle at an angle into the body pointing into the arm. Push fibers from the body into the arms.

Attach the legs to the other end of the body in the pose that you want the bear to have. Fan out the wool at the end of the leg and wrap it around the body, shallowly needle felting the loose fibers. Attach the legs the same way you attached the arms. Poke from the body into the legs and then from the legs into the body.

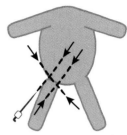

Bear parts needled together and covered.

Wrap with the Cover Wool After the Parts are Attached Together When the arms, legs, and body are together, add the cover fiber where the arms and legs were attached and over the body if the core fiber is showing. Place a thin layer of cover fiber over the areas of attachment to hide them and needle them down. Hold two or three of the smallest needles (40-gauge or 38-gauge star blade) and go over the whole surface of the body to secure the cover fiber, only poking $1/8$ to $1/4$ inch into the body. Take strips of brown wool to wrap around the bear. Needle the end of a strip to the bear. Hold it down flat and needle felt the strip onto the body. Gradually cover the bear with the brown wool, adding thin layers to spots where the core fiber shows through.

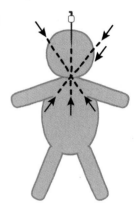

Use extra brown wool to build up different parts of the bear, the belly, for example. Use the needle to make indentation lines on the surface, adding definition to the body.

Bear's Head Roll a round ball for the head using your cover fiber. Finish most of the details on the head before you attach it to the body. Using the cover wool make a snout for the bear by making a little ball and needling it on using one of the finer needles. Make a black nose. Eyes can be a colored dot with a black dot inside. Place the head on top of the body and attach it to the body by poking the needle into the top and sides of the head and into the body, then from the body into the head.

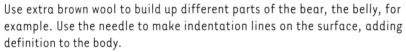

Make the Bear's Ears Last Make round ears for the bear. Pinch off some wool about the size of a nickel. Make the round outline of the bear's ear inside the wool then fold the wool outside the line over the ear. Leave a little wool not folded over to attach the ear to the head. 🐻

Building a Face

The parts of the face are built up in a specific order following steps where each feature builds on the next. Sculpting a face using this technique is one of the most unique uses for the felting needle.

PROJECT 4

Sun Face Sculpting on a Flat Surface Using the Felting Needle

Materials One ounce of core fiber. One ounce of cover fiber (gold or yellow wool) and colors for the eyes, mouth, and cheeks. Needles and foam work surface.

1. Use the 38-gauge or 38-gauge star needles to build up a base for the sun face. Make a 4-5 inch round pile of core wool on top of your foam work surface. Needle the wool onto the foam until it is about ½ inch thick.

2. Use about one ounce of cover wool to make the sun face. Half of the wool is for the rays and the other half is to build up the face.

3. Separate the wool into about ten, 2-inch long tufts for the sun rays. Twist one end of each piece to make it pointed. Fan out the other end, overlapping it onto the base. Lightly needle the rays to the base and to the foam.

4. Needle a thin layer of sun color wool on top of the circle. Now you are ready to build up the face. Listed are three wool arrangements used for sculpting the face.

Triangle-Shaped Rolled Strip (for chin and nose)

Hold the strip of wool in your two hands. Tightly roll the wool down toward you starting at the top. Fold in the two sides to make a triangle shape where you rolled. Keep rolling and folding in the sides until you have the size chin or nose you want for your face. Leave some loose wool hanging from the bottom of the triangle, and needle the triangle so it holds its shape.

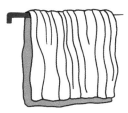

Folded Layer (for lips, eyebrows, and cheeks)

Layer a strip of wool that is wide enough for the mouth or cheeks. Fold the wool over a felting needle. Slip the needle out and needle felt the edge for lips. Cheeks and eyebrows are placed on the face without needling the edge.

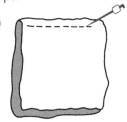

Small Pile of Wool
(to build up bridge of the nose and forehead)

Layer a pile of wool where the bottom is smaller than the top. Start with a small layer and gradually make the pieces bigger until the top piece covers the pile. Place the pile on the sun face where you want to build up the surface.

side view

Top view

Making the Face
Attach the main parts of the face using the 38-gauge triangle or star needle, just needling enough to place the parts. After the parts of the face are arranged, use the 38-gauge star needle to secure the surface. Use the 40-gauge for attaching the eyes and making fine lines. Secure the entire surface holding two or three 38-gauge star needles together. Read about seamless attachments and contouring attachments (Page 4.)

Chin Make a triangle-shaped roll of wool leaving about 1 inch of the end loose. Needle felt the triangle so it stays together. Place it on the bottom of the sun as shown with the loose end extending up and lightly needle felt it down into the base wool.

Nose Make a larger triangle shaped roll for the nose leaving 1½ inch of the end loose. Pull some wool down on each side for nostrils, and needle felt the nose so it holds together. Place the nose near the middle of the face with the loose wool extending up. Needle on each side of the nose behind the nostrils to attach it to the base. Needle felt a seamless attachment with the loose wool.

Mouth Upper Lip: Make a folded strip as wide as the mouth will be. The corners of the mouth should align to the middle of each eye. Place the strip on the foam and needle in the middle right at the fold leaving about ½ inch on each side. Gently pull the loose fibers apart and slip the top lip under and around the nose. Needle the lip in place on each side of the nose leaving the bottom loose under the nose. Needle a thin layer of light brown or peach-color wool onto the base wool underneath the lip.
Lower Lip: Make the bottom lip in the same way as the top lip. Place it under the top lip at the outside edges and let the loose wool extend down over the chin, then needle it in place on the edges and at the corners of the mouth.

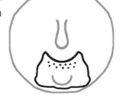

Cheeks Make two folded strips for the cheeks but don't needle the edge. The strip should go from the corner of the eye to the corner of the mouth close to the nose. Pull off some of the wool if it is too wide. Needle the two ends first, and then needle the cheek lightly in place. Place a thin layer of wool over the folded edge to hide it before securing it with the 38-gauge star needle.

Bridge of Nose and Eyebrows Layer a small pile of wool and place it over the top of the nose for the bridge. Needle it in place. For more distinct brows, make two folded strips and place them in the eyebrow area before you make the eyes. Place a thin layer of wool over the folded area to make it blend in with the face.

Eye Use the 38-gauge needle to make a needled outline for each eye. See the two suggested ways to make eyes in the illustration. Use the 38-gauge star or 40-gauge needle to attach the parts of the eyes.

Details The final details you add to your sun mask will give it personality. Use the 38-gauge star or 40-gauge needles for attaching the details to the face.

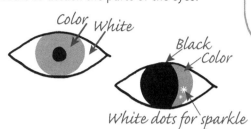

Color / White

Black

Color

White dots for sparkle

Roll two small strips of gold wool between your fingers and place one on top of each eye, covering it slightly, for eyelids.

Make two tiny balls of brown wool and needle them into the bottom of the nose for nostrils.

Needle a thin patch of pink or peach colored wool onto the upper part of each cheek to make rosy cheeks.

Accent the eyes with a very thin line of brown wool under and over each eye. Put a thin line of brown wool ½ inch over the eye to mark the eyelid. Poke the needle into one spot on the chin, over and over, to make a dimpled chin.

Add other lines or details to make your sun face come to life!

Needle Felt the Finished Sun Face Hold two or three 38-gauge star needles together and shallowly needle felt over the surface of the face poking only ⅛ to ¼ inch into the surface. Remove the sun face from the work surface by carefully peeling it off, starting at the top. Needle felt the core fibers on the back to flatten them without pushing the needle through the front of the face. Place strips of the sun color wool over the core fiber and needle felt it to make a smooth surface. Hang up the sun face and impress your friends!

Needle-Felting Techniques with Linda Van Alstyne

Now that you have gained some experience working with the felting needle, it is time to try a human figure. Using these original techniques developed by Linda Van Alstyne, try needle-felting a human figure. Needle felted designs on pages 32-41 by Linda Van Alstyne.

Needle Felt a Human Figure

An endless cast of characters can be created using needle felting techniques. All sculptures begin with a skeleton of some shape. The basic shapes of rolls and balls can be needled together in many positions.

When starting out it is important to determine how much fiber you will need by defining the size of the sculpture you want to make. Start small for your first project. Sketch your figure to your intended finished size, but keep in mind that the core fiber skeleton should be 25 to 30% smaller than your intended finished size. The basic shapes you form out of core fiber will increase in size as you add to them. The head will increase more than any other part of the figure. All other parts will also increase in size, as they are finished with cover fiber. This is because all the features of the sculpture are added onto the basic shapes.

Divide the Fiber Batt Divide the fiber you plan to use into the necessary components of the figure. The following is a simple division for a basic human form. It is only a guideline.

- Take the amount of core wool you will use for the figure. Divide the wool in half.
- Take one of the halves and divide it into a $^2/_3$ piece and a $^1/_3$ piece. Divide the $^1/_3$ piece in half again.
- The $^2/_3$ piece will be the trunk. Half of the $^1/_3$ will be the head, the other half is for building up the buttock, belly, etc.
- Divide the other half into $^1/_3$ for the arms and $^2/_3$ for the legs. Each of these 2 sections is divided in half again to make symmetrical arms and legs.

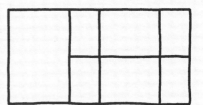

Dividing a Batt.

Form Basic Shapes Roll the core fiber batts into basic shapes for the body parts (see Chapter 4.) Lay out the core fiber batts for the body parts. Arms and legs can be made in two parts if they are bent at the elbow and knee or one long roll if the figure will be standing with arms and legs straight. One roll is made for the trunk. The head is a ball. The neck, hands, and feet are made from cover fiber. The contouring of the body can be done with cover fiber as you wrap the pieces.

Spread wool from one shape around the other.

Connect the Shapes The desired shape and position of the figure determine how you attach the arms and legs. The attachment can lengthen or shorten the leg depending where you overlap and attach the loose fibers from one roll onto the second roll.

> **Legs** Attach onto the outside of the torso or the end of the torso depending on whether you want to achieve wide or narrow hips.

> **Arms** Attach to the upper back to form a more rounded posture, or on the top edge of the torso to form a more shapely shoulder. If the character is reaching over the head, be sure to attach the arm to the body at that angle. Leave the ends of the fiber of the arms and legs loose for attachment of hands, feet, claws, etc.

Leg attached at side of trunk.

"Diaper" Batt Fill in the area where the legs attach to the torso by wrapping a diaper batt around the figure. This smoothes the area, adding volume more easily than wrapping. Overlap the front and back at the sides and needle the diaper onto the figure.

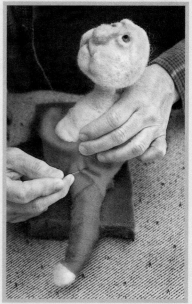

"Diaper" Batt.

Cover the Figure with a Layer of Colored Fiber First decide what color your figure will be and what it will wear. Choose wool in the colors for the outside layer. Separate the wool into narrow strips with consistent density. Wrap thicker areas first. If arms and legs are fleshy, begin wrapping up toward the torso. Loosely needle one end of a strip onto the figure. Pull the strip firmly and overlap the edges on each rotation to secure them. When wrapping, pull the fiber taut. This will make the fibers lay down smoothly and evenly. If too loose, they will pucker and pouch requiring much more needling to make a flat, finished surface. Make sure the strip of cover fiber is not too wide for the area you are covering or the edges will roll and not lay smooth. The tighter you wrap, the smoother the finish will be and the less needling will be needed to finish the piece. When you come to the end of a strip, gently needle it to secure the end fibers. Attach another strip of cover fiber, and needle the loose fibers to hold it in place.

When wrapping the knee and the elbow, form a figure eight around the joint. Start at the thigh or the arm, needle the end of a fiber strip to attach it to the top surface of the thigh (or arm). Wrap one half of the thigh (or arm), pulling the fiber strip behind the knee (or elbow), around to the front of the leg (or fore arm), back behind the joint to the starting point. Needle this cover

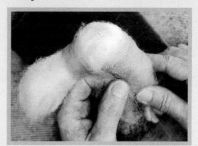

Figure eight around knee.

fiber shallowly to attach it to the core fiber. Make a knee cap or elbow by rolling a small ball. Leave loose fibers at one end of the batt. Lay the ball on the joint with the loose fibers lying smoothly over the thigh or arm. Needle the loose fibers using an invisible attachment. Next, work around the edge of the ball to attach it using a defined attachment technique. Build more contours to the calf or thigh, arm or fore arm, by tightly wrapping small strips of fiber around the upper end to make it thicker. Lightly jab the cover fiber in place with a 38-gauge triangle or star needle.

Make Hands and Feet Hands and feet are usually made last. They are made with the cover fiber using the 38-gauge star or 40-gauge needle. Needle shallowly because if you penetrate the needle through the finger or toe and out the other side, they will become very hairy and unsightly.

Cover joined area and needle to attach.

Hands Fingers can be made separately then needled to a small ball. Another way to make a hand is by making a mitten. Fold a thick yet narrow section of fiber in half and needle it slightly firm with loose fibers on one end. Needle inward along the edges to make them even and smooth. Attach the mitten to the forearm by separating the loose fibers and placing the end of the forearm between the fibers. Needle to attach but do not needle too deeply.

Cover the joined area with a strip of fiber. Tightly wrap the strip of fiber around the joined area and needle it securely but not too deeply. Make fingers by cutting with scissors lengthwise into the mitten and wrapping the cut ends with fiber. Needle each section to attach the fiber and to shape the fingers. Fingers can also be made individually around a bamboo skewer or thin wire and attached to the hand. Finish each finger separately shaping the tip and shallowly needling along the edges to smooth the fiber. Keep loose fibers at the other end for attachment onto a palm-sized mitten. Finger placement on the hand may vary depending on the hand position: open, spread fingers, closed fingers, etc.

Feet The foot is made in a similar way to the hand, except it is attached at a 90-degree angle to the lower leg. Add a small ball for the heel and a small roll for the ball of the foot. Make short, vertical cuts into the foot for toes. Wrap them and finish them as with fingers. If you don't want to make feet, you can make shoes by wrapping the foot shape with cover fiber in a chosen color. Add a heel to the shoe or boot and a small cone to the tip of the shoe to make it pointed. Add a small round ball to make it rounded. I usually make the shoes or boots last. If the foot is wearing a sock, cover the foot in the appropriate color before adding the shoe.

Needlefelt a Three-Dimensional Head

Use core fiber to form the ball for the head. The ball will be smaller than one would imagine for the head in relation to the trunk. This is because you will cover the ball with cover fiber and then build the features of the face onto it somewhat like a clay artist builds features with clay. As you work the head becomes larger. When you form the ball for the head, make sure to bring the sides in and rotate the ball as you roll, to keep it somewhat round. When it is tightly rolled, hold it on the sponge between your thumb and fingers of one hand and jab deeply into the center to entangle the loose ends. Rotate the ball while you are jabbing it to avoid flattening it. If the ball was tightly rolled and needled it should feel like a firm sponge. Too much needling on the surface will make it difficult to add features onto it. ✿

Form the Head Cover the ball with the color fiber you choose for the outer skin. This is where your creativity comes in. You can combine several colors to achieve more muted or interesting skin. Combine colors by carding or combing them together using hand carders. When you have the color you want, pull the fibers into a narrow strip. Fasten the end into the head and begin to wrap the head tightly, pulling the narrow strip taut as you rotate the ball. When you reach the end of the strip, needle it slightly to hold it in place and add another strip where you left off. Overlap the strips slightly to be sure to cover the core fiber.

Finish the face last after the body is completed. Creating heads with faces is so much fun that you can easily end up with a lot of heads waiting for bodies.

Wrap the ball with cover fiber.

Use the cover wool to make the smaller shapes that make up the facial features outlined below. I prefer to use coarse wool for the cover fiber because it tends to be easier to work with and covers the figure more evenly. Also the needle holes do not show on the surface of the figure.

The Face A human face follows certain rules of balance. (See illustration on page 29.) The eyes sit just above a horizontal line that divides the head in half. The nose rests just below this line. The centers of the eyes line up with the corners of the mouth. The attachment of the upper part of the ear is in direct line from the center of the eye. The lower ear attachment may vary in line from the bottom of the nose to just above the lip. A younger person and a baby have a flatter nose bridge and the eyes are farther apart. Corners of baby's lips may line up with the inner corner of the eye and this dimension changes as they age and grow. Though placement of each feature is important, dimensions of the face vary from person to person. Study facial features and you will see the differences. The eyes may be large and almond or round and beady. The nose may be bulbous, pug, pointed, or flared. The chin — broad, wide, long, pointed, doubled, or dimpled. Cheeks may sit high, sag, bag slightly, or greatly. Lips may be narrow, pursed, full, round, or flat. If you are considering a caricature, then any one or all of these features may be exaggerated. Experiment with the following techniques for making facial features.

Nose Make a small batt of cover fiber. Make this nose in proportion to the head. It is small. Roll it tightly and needle it lightly so that it stays in a roll. Fold up one end of the roll $1/3$ and needle to attach it to the roll. Place this nose on the face so that the fanned fibers lie just above an imaginary center line around the head and the ball of the nose lies just below this line. Attach the loose fibers to the forehead using an invisible technique. Once all of the loose fibers are secured to the head, needle at a perpendicular angle to firmly attach these fibers to the head. Next, lightly jab along both sides of the nose making an invisible attachment to the head. Hold the tip of the nose off the face while placing the needle at the base of the nose. Make deep jabs under the nose connecting it to the head projecting up from the face. Shallow indentations can be made on either side of the bottom of the nose to form nostrils. Define eye sockets by jabbing close to either side of the nose to depress the wool fibers. Then, make indentations further out from the bridge of the nose to form eye sockets. These indentations do not have to be deep, just enough to define placement of the eyes.

Chin Make another small batt of cover fiber for the chin. The batt of wool for the chin is thicker or denser in the center than the sides. As it is rolled it forms a crescent shape with thinner sides. The center should be rolled very tight, while loose fibers are jutting out from the thinner ends. Do not roll the entire batt, but leave a few loose fibers along the entire edge. The loose ends serve as attachment points. There should be loose fibers at each side of the chin and also pointing down toward the bottom of the face. Place the chin on the face along the bottom of the ball for a long face, or jutting out from the bottom edge of the ball for a pointed chin. Pinch the chin roll narrowly when attaching it to make it longer and more pointed, or spread it out to the far edges of the face to make the face more round. Attach the two thin ends to the ball using light deliberate jabs. Use the 38-gauge needle here. Once secure, wrap the remaining loose fibers along the bottom edge under the ball and needle them with light deliberate jabs to attach it firmly to the head. The upper edge of the chin serves as attachment point for the lower lip.

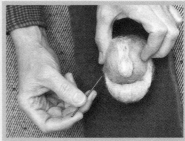

Place crescent roll chin under ball. Needle sides and back.

Upper and Lower Lip Make a small batt and needle across the center of it lightly. Fold it in half along this line. Needle the folded batt lightly along the half of the batt closest to the fold line. Once it is needled together, pick it up and separate the loose fibers, spreading them apart. Attach this piece to the bottom of the nose, so it is slightly hanging off the nose. Roll a small batt around a skewer, leaving some fibers loose at one edge. Remove the skewer, and attach along the lower

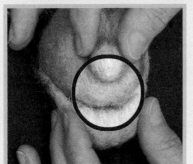

Upper lip wraps around nose.

chin line. Remember that adult lips reach from the center of one eye to the center of the other eye. Attach only at the corners of the lips. Bring down the upper lip and attach over the bottom lip forming the corners of the mouth. The shape of the lips can be formed open, smiling, sneering, pouting, or frowning, when attaching the upper lip corners to the lower lip corners.

Make a small ball from cover fiber and place it under the loose fibers of the lower lip edge. Pull the lower lip fibers over this small ball and attach to the chin. This adds contour to the chin. Use the 38-gauge needle and needle the loose fibers over the ball without flattening out the ball. Very, very small bits of colored fibers can be mixed to color the lips. The fiber is hand blended in your fingers and then the fibers are broken into very small bits. These small pieces are laid over the lips for color and shading. Use the 40-gauge needle to attach the colored fibers to the lips.

Lower lip wraps over chin.

Cheeks Make two small batts of cover fiber. Roll each batt tightly pushing both edges in towards the middle, but do not form a tight ball. Leave loose fibers at one end for attachment to the head. For high cheeks, place the ball next to the nose with the loose fibers pointing downwards and towards the outside of the face. For baggy cheeks, place the ball so the loose fibers point upwards and the ball is low on the face. Needle the cheeks on using the 38-gauge needle. Use an invisible attachment on the loose fibers and a defined edge along the contoured edge of the cheek. You will need to angle the needle along this finished side in order to avoid flattening the edge and making an obvious seam.

Needle a line for sagging cheeks.

Eyes Place the eyes close to the nose bridge on either side. Use the star blade needle here. Fill the eye indentations with white fiber. Don't be afraid to overfill the area. When the eyelids are added, they will make the eyes more proportional. Needle a small pupil in the center. I usually make this oval, but you can experiment with the shape. Work color on either side of the pupil. Use the 40-gauge needle to add a very, very small white dot where the pupil meets the iris. This can be anywhere along the join. The placement of the pupil, iris, and small white dot can make the eye look to one side or the other, up, down, or cross-eyed. Make small rolls for the bottom eyelids. Lay roll across the bottom of the eye. Needle to attach edges to inside and outside corners of the eye. Needle along bottom edge to attach to face.

Tear wool fibers apart to make short pieces for eye parts.

Make the top eyelid by laying down a small strip of wool the width of the eyelid. Fold one end over flat, and continue folding two or three times until just wisps of loose fiber remain. Needle it slightly to make it denser and needle from the folded edge inward to firm this edge up. Eyeliner color attaches easier if the edge is needled.

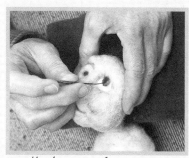

Needle the parts of the eye together.

Attach it to the face with the loose fibers oriented toward the forehead. Needle first at each corner, then work the loose fibers into the forehead. A larger half roll can be attached above the eyes to form a more prominent forehead. Attach it first to each side of the head and then work the loose fibers into the top of the head.

Ears Make crescent-shaped rolls for the ears. Roll tightly, but leave loose fibers at the ends and at both edges of the roll. Secure one end of the roll to the ball and then curve the roll into the shape of the ear that best suits the character. Attach the other end, and then needle the loose fibers along the long edge of the roll into the side of the head, making a deep indentation. This forms the inner canal of the ear. To make a sharp pointed ear, roll the fiber around a fine floral wire leaving the loose ends and edges as described above. When attaching the ear to the head, pinch the wire to shape the pointed ear.

Form a Neck You can choose to attach the head directly to the trunk, or form a neck. If making a separate neck, use the cover color and make a very short tight roll with loose fibers on both ends. Needle the center of the roll from both ends, leaving the end fibers loose and flared. This will tighten and shorten the neck. The flared edges will be needled to the head and the trunk for attachment. Using the 38-gauge needle, attach one flared end to the head, working from the neck into the head and the head into the neck.

Attach the other end to the trunk. Spread the flared end around and over the top of the trunk. Remember you can angle the head on the trunk so that the character is looking to the side, upwards, etc. Angle the needle (but do not bend the needle) and jab deeply from the trunk through the neck into the head, and then from the side of the head through the neck into the trunk. I always finish the head and shape the body before attaching the two together. Add the hair after the head is attached to the body. If you plan to add embellishments to the head or the body, do it before connecting the two. This avoids excess handling in awkward positions.

Attach the neck to the head.

Embellishments can be added later if you feel your figure needs them (beading, additional clothing, cording, wings, etc.).⚓

Needle-Felting Tips from Linda

When wrapping your figure either with core wool or cover fiber, keep the wool in an even strip and do not allow the strip of wool to twist or roll. If it twists it will not lay flat and will form ridges. This makes it more difficult to cover the piece evenly making it require more intensive needling.

Clothing can be Needled On in Many Ways The cover fiber can be the clothing, *(e.g. pants, shirts, bathing suits, shoes, socks, and hats.)* For loose or three-dimensional clothing, make thin felt using the wet felting technique. Leave one edge half-felt, and apply it by needling the soft edge. When using fabric yardage, place the piece of fabric on the body and cover the edge of the fabric with fiber. Needle through the fiber into the body to attach the fabric. This makes a fine attachment for a skirt, apron, or wings made from stiffened fabric. Lightweight silks, rayon, cotton gauze, or tulle can be needled on the figure for clothing.

Half-felt pieces can be needled onto the figures to make polka dots, stripes, etc. Shirt stripes, edges of vests, the neck of a sweater, and cuffs can also be added to the figures in half-felts. Needle singles yarn at edges of clothing to define vests, coats, and necklines.

Add Depth to your Figure Through Shading and Color This is the secret to sensational figures. Use bits of colored wool to color the face and create depth in creases. Work fine, not heavy, with detail lines. For rouge, break longer fibers into shorter pieces by tearing them apart to make very, very thin layers. Place these on the cheeks, nose, and chin. Combine more than one color to give a realistic effect.

Add a fill color to the inside of the mouth (if it is open) using a dark color such as brown rather than red. It gives more depth to the face. Color effects can also be achieved by hand carding several colors together. These small batts can then be used as cover fiber.

Use your imagination to create teeth, finger and toenails, and hair. For teeth, use very small balls or very thin rolls. Needle them under the upper lip line and above the lower lip line. If using thin rolls, needle into the roll forming indentations to define teeth. Add bits of colored wool to the ends of fingers and toes to form nails.

There is no right or wrong in dry needle felting. Experiment and see what works for you. Once you become comfortable using the needles and joining the pieces, you can create any form you can imagine. Enjoy!

Wet with Dry Felting Techniques

The possibilities for combining wet and dry felting techniques are endless. This Fairy Doll project guides you through the process for making a doll you can pose using needle-felting techniques. The surface and clothing are then wet felted to give a different surface texture to the finished project. Embellishments can be added as desired. The Nisse or Scandinavian Elf project combines needle felting with wet felting. The cone-shape is needle-felted together, then the outside layer is wet felted to form a skin. After the cone dries the face is sculpted by needle felting on the surface.

Fairy Doll

Materials

Two 12-inch pipe cleaners, flesh-colored wool, wool for clothing, a small bowl of warm water, and a bar of soap. (Before wet felting, melt bar soap in a small amount of very hot water to make a thick gel.)

1. **Make the Wire Skeleton** Bend one of the pipe cleaners in the middle. Twist the ends making small circles for feet. Take the other pipe cleaner and make a small loop in the middle the size of a quarter. Twist the ends to make small circles for the hands. Place the end of the leg pipe cleaner through the loop for the head and twist together to finish the skeleton.

Pipe cleaner skeleton.

2. **Wrap the Skeleton with Wool** Wrap thin strips of flesh-colored wool evenly around the skeleton. Start at the neck then go down the arms. Twist around the body and down each leg. Make the thickness $3/8$ to $1/2$ inch of wool. Bend the wire at the shoulders, elbows, knees, feet, and hands.

Wool wrapped skeleton.

3. **Make the Head** Roll a small ball and needle it slightly. Push it into the head loop. Wrap a thin strip of wool around the head to cover the pipe cleaner loop and needle it.

4. **Make a Face** Build up a face as described in the Sun Face instructions. Make the pieces very tiny and needle them onto the head. Start with the chin. Then add the nose, upper lip, lower lip, and cheeks if necessary. The Fairy has a child's face. Keep the eyes lower and slightly larger and wide apart. Make a tiny nose and a mouth.

5. **Fingers, Toes, and Hands** (See page 35) To make individual fingers, first make a thumb by rolling a small bit of wool and only turning in one side of the roll so the fibers on the other side stay loose. Wrap a little extra wool around the hand to make a mitten. Make only two cuts, giving the hand three fingers and a thumb. Wrap the fingers with a tiny bit of wool and needle them. Needle the thumb onto the hand. Add a strip of wool around the thumb where it attaches to the hand. Needle it together. Make toes, or cover the feet with slippers in a contrasting color.

You can continue and add clothes to the fairy now, then wet felt everything together, or you can wet felt the skin of the fairy first, following the instructions in Project #2 for wet felting the surface of the star. Gently work over the face and hands. If you choose to wet felt now, don't rinse out the soap, allow the fairy to dry a little before adding the clothing.

6. **Fairy Clothes** Fairies wear delicate clothing. Several ways to make clothes are discussed on page 41, "Needle Felting Tips From Linda." The following steps are for felting the clothes directly onto the doll.

Wrap the Wool Around the Doll Take a thin strip of wool in the clothing color for the fairy and wrap it securely over the shoulders, crossing from front to back. Wrap down and around the arms for a short- or long-sleeve top. Continue wrapping — but this time loosely — around the waist and down the legs to make a skirt. The wool will shrink when you felt it.

Wet Felt the Clothing Splash a little hot water over the doll then dip your fingers into the soap gel and pat it onto the doll's clothes. The soap gel will make the wool lie flat so the fibers won't stick to your fingers as you press on them. If you find that the fibers are sticking to your hands, use more soap gel or press more gently. With your thumb and index finger on either side of the body gently rub and squeeze the clothes all over the body. Press the skirt between your fingers. Dip your fingers into the soap and add more water if needed. After several minutes the wool will form a soft felt. Keep rubbing until you see the clothes have shrunk and the felt is stiff.

Let the doll dry for a day or two, then rinse out the soap under a gentle spray. Drip-dry the doll. When the doll is dry you can needle hair on it and sew or glue on wings or other embellishments. For a flower fairy, place a felt flower on her head.

7. **Fairy Wings** Wings can be made in many ways with a variety of materials. Heat bondable iridescent fiber can be made into wings. Scatter the fiber between two sheets of tissue paper. Set your iron on silk setting and briefly iron over the top sheet of paper to bond the fiber to itself. Cut out wings, and glue or sew them onto the back of the doll between the shoulders. Or make a felted "sandwich" with the bonded fiber as the middle layer and very thin layers of wool on one or both sides. Gently wet felt the sandwich using the rolling in bubble wrap technique (See page 20).

- Bend thin plastic coated floral wire into wings then wrap it with merino wool and wet felt it following the above technique for wet felting the clothing.

- Make needle-felted wings onto a foam work surface. (See Project #2.)

A Scandinavian Elf or "Nisse"

with Patricia Spark *Scandinavian Nisse by Patricia Spark.*

Materials Core fiber for the inside. Fine or medium fine wool that felts well by the wet method for the outside "skin" layer. Flesh color for the face, and red or blue for the hat. The coat can be another color. Locks of white curly fiber for the hair and beard. Use a 36-gauge triangular blade for gross shaping. For detail work first use a 38-gauge triangular blade and then a 38-gauge star blade and 40-gauge for finer detail. Use a large tapestry needle to pull up the fiber for sculpting the face.

1. Felt base Lay out a batt of core fleece approximately 6" x 12". Lay another strip of wool about 3" x 12" over the bottom of this batt. (The batt sizes can vary in order to make differently sized cones.) Roll the batt tightly into a cone shape, with a broad base and a narrow, pointed top. The extra fleece added to the bottom of the carded batt will make it easier to form this cone. Place the cone on a piece of foam rubber and jab the shape with the needle until it begins to firm up. Move the needle all over to make the core firm up uniformly in all areas.

2. Outside Felt Skin, Colored Face, and Hat Lay a strip of flesh-colored wool fiber around the base, just above the mid-point. Needle it into position with the 38-gauge triangular blade. Place a strip of red fiber above this flesh-colored strip to form the pointed hat. Needle it into position. Needle another color beneath the flesh-colored fiber for the elf's coat.

3. Felt the Skin Quickly dunk the needled shape into cool, soapy water. Do not leave it in the water. Put soapy water on your hands and begin to rub and massage the shape with your hands until a felt skin forms on the outside. Let the elf dry. After it is dry, rinse the shape well with a light spray of water. Roll in a towel and fluff it up a bit to get back its shape. Let it dry. You can now use the needles to add the facial features, and hair to the elf shape.

4. Face Use the tapestry needle and the 38-gauge star and 40-gauge felting needles to sculpt the face. Poke the tapestry needle into the face in the nose area and pull up the wool to make a bump for the nose. Poke the 38-gauge star needle into each side to sculpt and shape the nose. Pull up fiber for a chin, lips, and cheeks, and then needle at an angle to the face to define these features. If you think the nose should be larger, add a ball of wool and needle felt it onto the face. Poke an outline for the eyes and add the parts of the eye as outlined in the previous sections. You can add definition to the face as you poke with the finer felting needles, sculpting out cheeks, etc. Add color to the cheeks and inside the mouth by needling on colored fibers or shade lightly with pastels.

5. Hair Needle on locks of curly fiber for the beard and hair. You're done!

More Fun Projects

Brief instructions for some of the projects pictured on the front and back covers and inside of the book are outlined below. Most of the detailed instructions for the techniques are in the text of the book. More instructions for wet felting can be found at the North American Felters Network website at www.peak.org/~spark/feltmakers.html and in the books listed in the Appendix.

Shooting Star Make a star by twisting three pipe cleaners to make five points. Wrap core wool around the center and each point to build up the star, needling the shape, then needle on cover wool for the star color. Use the cover wool to make a face. The "tails" that hang off the tips of the star are made as follows:

- Make a felt cord with the fibers left loose at one end.

- Needle the loose fibers onto the tips.

- Wet felt the surface of the star to blend in with the tails.

To make the felt cord for tails and other embellishments pull off a thin strip of the cover wool about 6" to 8" long and lay it on top of a 12" x 12" piece of $^3/_8$ inch bubble wrap with the bubble side up. (You can tape the bubble wrap to the work area.) Pile thin strips of wool to make a fluffy 6" to 7" long pile that is about $1^1/_2$ inch wide, lying lengthwise on top of the bubble wrap.

Dip your hand into the bowl of water. Hold your fingers together and press with your fingers and palm on top of the end of the pile of wool. While pressing down on the wool, move your hand back and forth until the wool under your hand contracts into a soft rope. Keep your quick back and forth gentle enough so that the roll holds together. Use more pressure as the wool contracts. When the end has formed a soft rope, move your hand down the roll to felt the next section. Keep working until you still have 2 to 3 inches of dry wool at the end of the roll. Continue to dip your hand in the water as you are working.

Rub some soap on your hand and roll the softly felted end over the bubble wrap with rapid back and forth movements. Dry your hands and add more dry wool to the other end of the rope if you want it to be longer. Wet your hand again and continue to felt the rope. Rub soap on your hands and felt the whole rope, holding the rope between your hands and rolling it to shrink it.

Make a twisted rope by wadding it up into a ball and adding warm water and soap. Then, while holding the bunched up rope between your cupped hands, move your hands against each other in a circular movement, squeezing and putting pressure on the rope. The rope will shrink and kink up during this process. Rinse the soap out and when you let the rope dry in the kinked up form, it will keep its shape.

Puffin Make a tube shape with a thicker area in the middle. Needle it onto a straight cylinder so it becomes a curved shape. Fill in the sides where the two pieces meet with two thin rolls. Place an oval sideways on the top for the head. Cover the core wool with black and white fiber and needle orange/red/yellow wool on the beak. Needle the wool onto the figure where it should be placed. Wrap pieces of wire with orange wool for the legs and webbed feet. Or make webbed feet by needling the shape over foam then needling them to the puffin.

Swan Make an oval for the body. Attach a long tube for the neck and head. Bend the tube at the end to form a head. Needle into the wool in the bent shape to make it stay bent. Make the top and bottom bill separately by needling them directly on the foam, leaving loose fiber on one end. Position the bill pieces and needle the loose fibers into the swan's head. Needle on brown spots for the eyes. Make two thin rolls and attach to the body on each side of the bottom to make the swan stand up. Needle two wings onto foam then attach to sides of body.

Fantasy Flowers Pinch off tufts of wool for five petals and place them together on your foam work surface. Put a contrasting color of wool in the middle. Needle a line for the edge of the petals, then turn the wool in at the edges to make a flower with five petals. Needle felt it enough so that it can be pulled off the work surface without pulling apart. Wet your hands and rub a little soap on them. Place the flower in the palm of your hand and press it with the fingers of your other hand, rubbing it in a circular motion until it is stiffly felted. The petals will stand up if you rub it around and around in your cupped hand. Make a group of flowers and rinse the soap out; let them dry; then sew or glue them onto a looped ribbon for a flower garland.

Lamb Make an oval for the body and four tube shapes for the legs. Make a smaller oval for the head. The ears are made on the foam work surface in a "u" shape with loose fibers at one end. Needle mohair locks onto the surface of the lamb.

Monkey Make long rolls for the arms and legs, two for each limb. Make a long oval body and a round head. Connect all the parts in the positions you want. Make a long cord for the tail. Make small ovals for the hands and feet. Tiny rolls are made separately and attached for fingers and toes. Add extra balls or folded batts of wool for the knee caps, the behind, the shoulders, or other areas. Cover the body with a colored layer and add a face, ears, and hair.

Tiny Animals Tiny animals can be built out of tiny rolls of cover wool that are needled together. The balls are then arranged in the animal shape and again needled together. Thin strips of wool are laid over the joints in the built-up body and needled on, resulting in a smooth outside layer.

Puppet Theatre Setting This project combines wet felting with needle felting to make a backdrop of laminated felt over cotton voile fabric. Start by laying down the fabric and laying down wool fiber in forest colors over it. Lay netting on top of the fabric. Wet down the wool with warm water that has a little soap added. Roll up the fabric in bubble wrap then roll it and re-roll it in all directions until the fiber begins to come through the fabric. After the backdrop is dry, needle felt details on. These include a little door in the trunk of the tree, mushrooms, flowers, and leaves. Needle felt wool into areas to fill in.

Make the tree by rolling core wool onto a skewer to create a cone shape. Needle felt individual boughs onto foam, leaving loose fiber on one end. The boughs are needle felted around the cone starting at the bottom to make a pine tree. Mushrooms are made to be free standing by layering a pile of wool, then placing several washers in the middle. Wrap up the wool around the washers and needle together to form a stem. Needle a cap of red wool to the top of the stem. Add tiny dots of white wool.
Puppets by Suzanne Down.

A Mask Needle-Felted onto a Background Fabric

Fantasy faces or animal faces can be used for the design of a needle-felted mask. Techniques for building a face are used to build up the mask onto a piece of fabric. You will needle punch the wool onto one half of the batting; then the other side of the batting is folded around the back of the mask and stitched down.

Follow these instructions to make a mask but choose the shape and colors you will use according to the character you are making.

Materials Foam work surface at least as large as the mask, a 10" X 20" piece of cotton batting or fabric, wool fiber in the colors of the mask and yarn.

1. Fold the fabric in half lengthwise and trace the mask shape onto the batting using a permanent marker. Your work area will be 10" x 10". Unfold the cloth and place the half with the traced pattern over a foam work surface. Use the 38-gauge star needle and needle-felt a thin layer of the background color of wool over the batting, inside the pattern line you drew.

Animal Mask Make fur going out on each side of the head. If the wool extends off of the fabric, needle felt it until it holds together. Make pointed or round ears, using a paper pattern and the steps from Project #2. Leave loose fibers on the bottom. Needle the loose fiber onto the mask in the appropriate place. The needle-felted ears will stand up, coming out from the mask surface.

Whiskers Make thin lines using black and white wool and place them on either side of the nose. Needle the lines into the wool and batting to form whiskers.

Mouth For a fierce animal such as a wolf, the bottom of the mask forms the mouth with teeth hanging down. Needle a thin line of black along the bottom of the mask. Then needle a row of white wool into the batting about $1/2$ inch wide. Cut out the teeth when you cut away the rest of the batting.

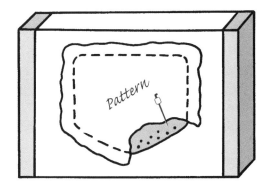

2. **Eyes** Cut eyeholes in a piece of paper and hold them up to your eyes to check for size and spacing. Center the paper over the mask where you want the eyes. Poke the felting needle through the eyeholes to mark where the eyes will be. Take away the paper and make a black outline around the eyes using black wool. Pull some fibers slowly out of a fluff of black wool and roll them between your thumbs and index fingers. When the thin roll holds together, lay it down on top of the edge of the eyeholes and needle it into the fabric.

3. **Nose** For a human, use the directions in project #4 to make the facial features. For an animal, form a triangle from black wool and needle it down at the bottom point of the mask where the nose should be. Needle a thin layer of darker wool for contrast over the nose and up the animal's snout.

4. **Final Needle-Felting** After all of the wool is laid out on the mask and needled down, the next step is to do a final needle felting over the whole mask. Hold two or three 38-gauge star needles together or use a multi-needle tool to make the process go faster The more needle punching you do, the smoother the surface will be. It is not possible to do too much needle punching. You don't have to needle inside the eyes and mouth because they will be cut out.

5. **Finishing the Mask** Slowly pull the mask off of the foam work surface. Look on the back to see the wool coming through the batting. Check for places that don't have as much wool coming through and needle these spots a little more.

Cut out the Eye Holes Make a cross cut in the wool and batting in the middle of the eye with a sharp, pointed scissors. Cut to the edge of the black wool then turn the mask over and cut the 4 flaps from the back. Trim the cut edges if the batting shows from the front. Cut the other eye.

Sew the Backing onto the Mask Fold the other half of the cotton batting over the back of the mask lining up the edges. You can pin the two sides together before you sew it. Use sewing thread that matches the background wool color. Sew around the edge of the mask, 1/4 inch inside the line. Use black thread to sew around the eyeholes. Cut holes in the back piece of batting for the eyes, nose and mouth. Trim off the extra batting around the mask as close to the wool as possible. If you needled on white wool for teeth, cut sharp teeth in a zigzag line.

Animal's Snout Fold the mask in half down the middle of the head. Now flatten the half beneath the eyeholes and you have formed the snout on the wolf. Thread a sewing needle; push the needle into the back of the mask, about two inches beneath the eyes and $1\frac{1}{2}$ inch from the fold. (See illustration) Push the needle through to the front of the mask; turn it then push it back again through the same spot. Repeat on the second side but leave one to $1\frac{1}{2}$ inch slack on the thread so the two sides are not tight together. Hold the mask up to your face. The thread going across should be right under your nose. Redo it if necessary and knot the thread when it is finished.

Make the Yarn Cord and Sew it onto the Mask Cut three $1\frac{1}{2}$-yard pieces (54 inches each) of yarn, preferably black. Lay the pieces side by side and have a friend hold one end. Twist the other end clock-wise until the yarn is tightly twisted but doesn't twist onto itself. While still holding the two ends, bring them together and let the yarn twist onto itself starting at the middle. The tightly twisted yarn will double twist onto itself forming the final sturdy multiple twisted cord. Knot the cut ends together. Sew the cord to the outside of one eyehole. Hold the mask up to your face and pull the cord around your head snugly. Hold it where you need to sew it onto the other side so it will stay on, with the cords resting on top of your ears to hold the mask up. Sew the second side and tie back any extra cord. Now your mask is ready to wear! ✿

Appendices An Overview of Felting Needles
by Linda Van Alstyne

Felting needles come in a variety of shapes and sizes. They are primarily used industrially in machines that hold thousands of needles in large flat plates. But in sculptural needle felting, they are used singly or in a hand held apparatus that may hold two or more needles. I prefer to use one or two when I am sculpting figures.

All felting needles have a basic shape. They have a long shank with a narrow shaft that has a very sharp tip. The shaft is barbed. A barb is an indentation, and it is this feature that catches the wool and enables you to felt. The number of barbs, the location, and the depth varies between needles. The smaller barb depth will push less wool and vice versa.

Let's look at these features and how they impact needle felting. A thin shaft of 38- or 40-gauge that is either star or triangular shaped will leave the least visible hole in the finished piece. The needle that has a shallow to a progressively deeper barb depth will leave an even smaller hole or visible sign in the finished piece. But when working with a needle with this progressive barb depth, felting will feel like it is going much slower than when using a needle that has deeper and more even barb depths. On most of the needles that felters are using today, the barbs start $3/8$" from the tip. I suggest using a needle with a barb starting only 3.2mm ($1/8$") from the tip because the needle edges do not have to penetrate very deeply to work effectively, and this feature gives the felter more flexibility. The needle can be used for shallow or deep work. A shaft that has barbs starting at 3.2mm from the tip and with barb depths progressively deeper along the shaft from the tip, will allow for very fine and shallow surface work, but also deep sculpting as the needle is pushed deeper into the wool. This needle construction is especially good for fine details such as making fingers, toes, eyes, and lips. Very little surface deformation occurs, as the needle does not have to go deep to push the wool. Also, when covering a sculpted base with an outer fiber, the needle only needs to penetrate to the depth of the first barb to connect the two surfaces and harden the top surface, leaving a very finished appearance. Further contouring is achieved by pushing the needle deeper into the piece to grab more wool.

The location of the barbs on the shaft can be very close together (clustered), or they can be staggered on each edge of the shaft. When the barbs are clustered at the same location on each edge of the shaft, the needle will push more wool at one time and a visible hole is made. This is a very aggressive needle. One such needle is the crown needle and some doll makers have used this to attach mohair "hair" to the dolls head. A needle with barbs staggered along the shaft will leave a smaller penetration hole because the wool is caught a bit at a time and the entanglement of the fibers is more gradual. The shape of the needle shaft is not always triangular. Most of the needles used today by hand felters have been triangular. Another needle style that has a great many applications for the needle felter has a star-shaped blade. This needle has eight barbs, two per shaft. This blade can be quite aggressive and still leave a very fine hole due to its unique shape. The conical-shaped blade leaves large holes and does not seem to be very effective with sculptural feltmaking with fine wool fibers. It may be of some benefit when adding pre-felts to a layout such as a rug. It will grab many more fibers and cause the pre-felt to attach to the background rather quickly. When felted with traditional techniques, the holes should disappear.

Four Needle Styles that I Prefer to Work With

1. 36-gauge triangular blade with barbs of equal depths, beginning at $3/8$" from the tip. This is an aggressive needle and is best suited for rough shaping the body of a needle-sculpted piece, or attaching them together. It does leave visible holes. It is also useful for attaching pre-felts to a background, or cording to a hat or mask.

2. 38-gauge triangle blade with varied barb depths, beginning 3.2mm from the tip. This allows you to work both shallow and deep, leaving hardly visible penetration holes. This is good for attaching the outer color fiber to the basic core structure. It will allow you to work both on the surface for finishing, yet let you go deeper for finish sculpting and posing the figure.

3. 40-gauge triangle blade that has varied depths, from very shallow to somewhat deeper, with barbs beginning 3.2mm from the tip, is the best for facial features. This includes working the fine detail in the eye and attaching lips without flattening or deforming them, then covering them with the outer fiber. I also find this needle useful when needling fiber onto very fine 3.5mm or 8.0mm silk. The needle marks are initially evident, but the weave threads of the fabric are not broken. Once wet felted, these marks disappear. This is useful in repair of a hole. This needle is also great for attaching seams of a garment, whether laminated or fine felt. It does not need to penetrate deeply to work and it has more edges for grabbing wool. These features speed up the joining process.

4. 38-gauge star blade with shallow barbs of the same depth that begin 3.2mm from the tip is great for rough shaping and fine work. Because of its shape (it has eight barbs, four per shaft edge), it pushes more wool and leaves very fine penetration holes. It can be used to attach needle-felted pieces together forming the basic sculptural shape and then covering it with the outer fiber. I also find this needle useful when needling fiber onto very fine 3.5mm or 8.0mm silk. The needle marks are initially evident, but the weave threads of the fabric are not broken. Once wet felted, these marks disappear. This is useful in repair of a hole. This needle is also great for attaching seams of a garment, whether laminated or fine felt. It does not need to penetrate deeply to work and it has more edges for grabbing wool. These features speed up the joining process.

Wool-Related Vocabulary

Carded Wool Wool fiber that has been processed by passing it through a carding machine that brushes the wool with metal teeth, thereby aligning the fibers in mostly one direction and removing dirt and debris from the wool.

Dyed wool Washed wool that has been colored in a dye bath and usually has been carded.

Felt A non-woven fabric.

Felting The process of making felt.

Locks Wool that is still in the same arrangement as it was on the sheep or other animal it came from (Breeds include Mohair Goats, Lincoln, Wensleydale, Border Leicester Sheep.) For needle felting the locks are gently washed and dyed but never carded. Locks are used for hair on sculptures.

Pre-felt (half-felt, soft-felt) Wool fibers that have been matted together to form a very soft fabric that can be pulled apart. A hard felt is formed when the pre-felt is fulled — rolled, agitated in a washer, or rubbed on a washboard using hot, soapy, water.

Unspun Wool Usually washed fleece that has been carded but has not been spun into yarn.

Wool Batts In wet felting these are piles of carded wool that have several layers where the fibers in alternate layers are lying cross-wise to each other. In dry felting a wool batt can be a strip of wool or several strips of wool layered on top of each other with the fibers in each layer lying in the same direction.

Wool Fleece The wool sheared from a sheep or wool fiber that has not been spun.

Sources for Supplies

Resource List for Feltmaking
Wet and Dry Felting Supplies *(Needles, Fiber, Locks, Tools, Kits, Books, and More.)*

FeltCrafts	www.feltcrafts.com	800-450-2723
Fine Fiber Press		541-917-3251
Fine Felt Farm	www.finefeltfarm.com	540-854-6081
Halcyon Yarn	www.halcyonyarn.com	800-341-0282
Liberty Ridge	www.libertyridgefarms.com	315-337-7217
Peace Fleece	www.peacefleece.com	800-482-2841
Susan's Fiber Shop	www.susansfibershop.com	888-603-4237
Woodland Woolworks	www.woodlandwoolworks.com	800-547-3725
The Woolery	www.woolery.com	800-441-WOOL

Multi-needle Tools

Celtic Moon Fibreworks	www.feltdesigns.com	604-462-8539

Fiber *(Additional Sources)*
Core Fiber Find out if there are sheep farmers in your area and ask for wool that will not felt using soap and water.

Cover Fiber *(See sources above, additional sources below.)*

Harrisville Designs	www.harrisvilledesigns.com	603-827-3333
Norsk Fjord Fiber	www.norskfjordfiber.com	828-884-2195
Wilde Yarns	www.wildeyarns.com	215-482-8800

Iridescent Fiber *(Heat Bondable)*

FeltCrafts	www.feltcrafts.com	800-450-2723

Needle-Punched Wool Batting

Taos Mountain Wool Works		505-776-2925

Books

The following resources for wet felting are available from your local bookseller, your public library or by calling the phone numbers below.

The Art of Feltmaking, Felting By Hand and ***Feltmaking Projects for Children*** by Anne Einset Vickrey

| FeltCrafts | www.feltcrafts.com | 800-450-2723 |

Feltmaking Techniques and Projects and ***Scandinavian-Style Feltmaking Techniques*** by Patricia Spark

| Fine Fiber Press. | | 541- 917-3251 |

Filt I Form and ***Sculpturel Filting*** (in Danish) by Brigitte Krag Hansen

| English translations available from Fine Fiber Press | | 541- 917-3251 |

Videos

Wet-Felting

Feltmaking: The Basic Process

and ***Feltmaking: Garments and Surface Design Techniques*** with Anne Einset Vickrey

| FeltCrafts | www.feltcrafts.com | 800-450-2723 |

Needle-Felting

Introduction to Needle Felting: Sculpting a Doll with Sharon Costello

| Black Sheep Designs | www.blacksheepdesigns.com | 518-797-5191 |

Needle felting supplies and kits are also available.

Online Needle-Felting Information

| North American Felter's Network | www.peak.org/~spark/feltmakers.html |

On-Line Needle-Felting Classes

Kathy Hays	www.craftycollege.com
Celtic Moon Fibreworks	www.feltdesigns.com
Birgitte Krag Hansen	www.feltmaking.com

Puppetry Art

Juniper Tree School of Story and Puppetry Arts

| P.O. Box 17666, Boulder, CO 80308 junipertreepuppets@hotmail.com | 303-776-0937 |

Kits and supplies for puppetmaking and storytelling. Call or write for free catalog.

- Jacket made with alpaca wool, life-size sheepdog, horse head by Wendy Wiebe
- Elephant and gargoyle by Linda Van Alstyne • Musicians "Making Music" by Sharon Costello
- Gnome and Mother Earth puppets by Suzanne Down

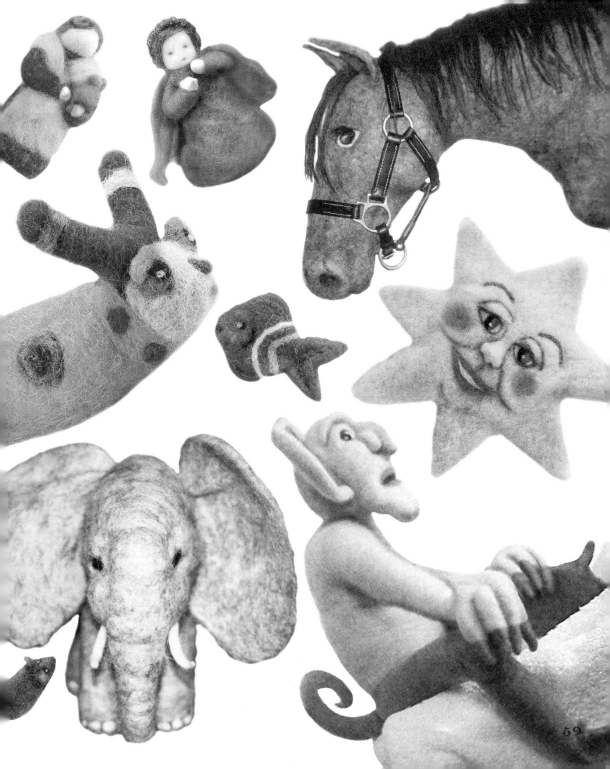

About the Author

Anne Einset Vickrey, an experienced teacher, author and designer, conducts workshops and writes articles about the craft of feltmaking. She has hosted two videos on the subject and created a line of feltmaking craft kits. Anne's work has been featured on "The Carol Duvall Show" (Home & Garden TV) and on "Home Matters" (Discovery Channel). In addition to Needle Felting Art Techniques and Projects, she is the author of three other books on Feltmaking. (See Appendix.) *Original needle-felted designs on the cover and throughout the book by Anne Einset Vickrey, except where credited to other artists.*

Contributors

Patricia Spark is a practicing artist with an MFA in Textile Design, whose areas include feltmaking, watercolor, monotypes and drawing. She has exhibited her artwork both nationally and internationally. She is an experienced teacher and the author of two books on feltmaking (See Appendix) and the translator for three books. She is currently the editor of the North American Felter's Network, a quarterly publication for felt enthusiasts.

Linda Van Alstyne is an experienced fiber artist in a variety of media, including spinning, weaving, and basketry. In 1996, she discovered the sculptural qualities of handmade felt, which allowed her to combine her love of fiber arts with her creative mask and caricature ideas. She has perfected her own technique for "needle sculpting" dry wool fiber into whimsical three-dimensional characters. Her research on felting needles provides the basis for the needles chosen for sculptural needle felting. Linda teaches her techniques nationally and internationally.

Acknowledgements

A special thanks to the following artists for contributing examples of their work. Sharon Costello of Black Sheep Designs, Suzanne Down of Juniper Tree Puppets, and Wendy Wiebe of Fine Felt farm.